First published in 2014
by

W   O
 space
R   D

an Imprint of Leeds Trinity University
Brownberrie Lane
Leeds LS18 5HD

Typeset by the author

A CIP record for this book is available from the British
Library

ISBN 978-0-9559004-3-3

'Algebra'

If a fifty-three year old woman
who lives halfway up a hill
leaves her house at 9 a.m.
to teach a 10.30 class
and walks three miles
(through four inches of fresh snow)
and half a mile on two inches of slush
(which contains 15% compacted ice)

and stops

twice

to listen to birdsong

how many calories does she burn
and what colour is the sky?

You should show your workings out.

'Driving Forces'

There's dignity in this desiccated skull,
pale sheep's head sinking into a lumpy field.
Perhaps her ancestors turned their narrow eyes
on Hadrian's soldiers, watched them obsessive
at their antlike tasks.
The fierce fear of the invader is urgent, wind-sharp.

The ridged horns wiggle in gloved hands
as I twist the strong curves under grey light.
There's some enduring potency in these firm lines
of nose bones stretching to the mandible,
and ancient rhythms in this fine zigzag fusing the skullplates.

The museum boasts a well-designed tool:
an archaeologist has labelled this grimy fragment.
Through the glass we read its function,
its reticence prised open,
and in the next case are empty leather strips
of Lucillus' boot, and threads of Maximilian's cloak
(but no bones – that would be too close for comfort).

Perhaps the legions longed for southern suns
to warm the stones and bronze their skin,
though some, of course, were born here -
bred the sheep, enslaved the untamed land.
On vacant folds of grazed hills
today's sheep ignore my pondering.
Scattered white bones record a common end.

'Cray'

In February, these stepping stones
clung on for dear life under a foot
of churning water. Sudden streams
arose for the hour;
the White Lion Pub perched itself
uneasily above the swollen brook.

Lambs buffeted blindly inside their dams.

Driven off the moorside
our feet were grounded on tarmac
beneath the busy waves.

Now, an afternoon on the cusp of summer,
gentleness has arrived.

The same lambs headbutt the air for kicks,
flicking neat ankles into the air.
The glistening road is silent, but the walls mutter
we have been here,
we have seen it all, so many times,
the silly sheep,
the sentimental urbanite
turned walker for a day.

'Humphrey Head'

Hungry, angry, loping to the furthest rim
of earth-meets-sky, the last grey wolf hunkers down.
His grizzled muzzle's stained
with recent chicken kill, teeth bared in rictus.

Righteous and brutal, but just as scared,
the hunter squats low in the reedbed.
He catches the feral smell of something
driven wilder to the edge of contested land.

Where should he seek? Inland, behind the leaning swathes
of trees, a lone thornbush steering into the wind,
each foot of rock kaleidoscoped with lichen
sharing the last foothold above the tideline.

Or facing outwards, back to the dense earth,
moving from solid to shifting, from stone to beguiling strands
neither sand not mud nor water but all three
silting and shimmering.

Sea-birds deposit webbed prints
as they dart across the elements
but neither the wolf nor the man has wings.

'Chi'

After a night spent skimming sleep like a swallow
the world seems glossed with a wobbly sheen.

Your hands and mine are stilled
round plates of cooling food. Between
fingers that may not touch
is the fizz of complex energies.

It seems I am auditioning
for a part in your life -
nothing as vulgar as chorus line,
but prompt, perhaps?

Surrounded by talkers, you talk, too,
of searching and reaching and touching,
describing such tenderness as would make
the angels weep.

From somewhere in limbo I listen.

'Vegetable love'

The great poets have said so much
about lovers parting for a while:
we've turned those pages side by side
and now our bodies read that loss.

Prefiguring it at dawn your hands
moulded themselves a memorial,
each mobile contour of my body fingered
into your primordial den.

I think of this when, after lunch,
I'm storing chitted potatoes
in cool, dark soil, the sun
a benison for my bending back.

'Book of Hours'

Layering two scripts together in midlife
created a palimpsest of desire
where your tight cursive lingered round
my looping hand
until the season when you awoke
and scratched out the manuscript
we were co-authoring, and
with a sharp click snapped shut
the gilt clasp on the tender vellum
of our first draft.

As the seasons cycle, I decide that next time
I'm tempted to transcribe a chapter
in the book of amours, I'd fare better
fooling around with some rude marginalia
like this priapic burgomeister, leering up
from the tail-end of 'September'
(spilling his cornucopia suggestively
at the foot of a vigorous – if leafless – tree),
his conk irreverently resembling the Duc de B's
and his brown hood slumped round his dewlap
in a manner which recalls Brother Sophronius,
about whose probity the Abbot, nightly, grieves.

'Mirror, mirror on the wall'

Not long before you started sleeping with our friend,
you gave me a full-length mirror.
Quite what masochism invited this request
I can't recall, as even then you'd started
to comment (ruefully) that bearing our kids
had left me a little thick round the middle.

Recently, I've stood before it (not always alone)
and interrogated my naked image,
marvelling how time folds experience
into such curves and angles.

Then did I see but in a glass darkly:
now, I behold myself face to face.

'On sleeping with cats'

Sometimes it's just your warm weight
pinning the duvet around my resting form,
anchoring me for the journey into night,
and when I stir in the darkness you mimic me,
lifting velvet heads for a sleepy caress.

Then a skittish mood takes you
and a stretched foot becomes prey.
You vocalise the task, and if
next door's stripy eunuch arrives
to share the play,
the full repertoire is performed -
the throaty growl, the tensed-up hiss -
vying with each other in defence.

You steal my sleep, my feline friends,
but if I trick you into leaving
my lady's chamber with handfuls
of malodorous crunchy things,
I lie awake, half-listening
for the approving purr,
my fretful fingers closing
on the remembrance of soft fur.

'Syntax'

In those last urgent days as sickness ate your life,
I browsed the Metaphysicals
pillaging conceits for comfort,
trying to decode the mystery of your dying.

I hoped some image could explain the paradox
of how we wanted you gone or back with us:
either, but not this limbo of child's dependence
without the hopeful vacancy of unscrolled years.

Your sated body prefigured an effigy,
the skin stone-hued and chilled.
Only the rasping breath conveyed
a symbol of life, not really your own.

Now your stilled body is both you and no-one.

So perhaps it is not breathing or its ceasing
which denotes living or not-living,
but your uniqueness, lost to us now
save through the reciprocity of prayer.

No metaphor helped, although
the grammar of mortality made sense:
your death is absence which reverses subject and object:
not 'She had cancer' but 'Cancer had her'.

'Discalced'

'He's fine,' your carer says,
'he's lost a shoe but happy going barefoot.'
I thank her and return to my meeting
distracted by the thought of you
steadying one foot at a time
on the fifteen treads of the stairs,
your toes leaning into the deep pile
as you go up then down because
you don't remember why up
or even what 'up' is.
          And I try to take an interest
in a smart spreadsheet,
pleased to think you'll be wearing socks
in a nice shade of fawn
(the colour of post-war frugality)
and that she made these for you,
fingers flashing the four silver spears
which clacked and chattered as she turned the heel
knitting her love into each pair,
something you can run your fingers over
because, now that words are treacherous,
textures console.
          And I plan to make for your birthday
a patchwork cushion from scraps
of warm Welsh wool, edged
with blanket stitch,
and I'll show your hands its narrative
of elusive shades from a forgotten land.
Suddenly this seems so much more urgent
than commenting on the coded cells
which populate the page -
a necessary ministry, a laying on of hands.

'Patricia'

When you're a ninety-two year old Byzantinist
the conference comes to you,
one snowy evening after the talking,
as a glass of red transferred carefully
into trembling, eager fingers
and a napkinful of pretzels
which you peck at between anecdotes,
blowing crumbs at me as I bend my ear to your tale.

Sixty years of conference wool on your back
you're no longer upright,
but your gaze is straight as an arrow
and your eyes bright, now with fun
as we agree being naughty is wasted on the young,
now with tears for your long gone husband.

An attendant daughter suggests I might want to circulate,
but I'm hooked: swapping stories about Brussels
(mine circa 1973, yours post-war),
and the joy of bearing children – and then it's time to go
and I press a kiss onto the soft crenulations of your cheek.
Your story warms me as I pick a route back
over the crusted ice of a reluctant spring.

'North front, floor four'

Sometimes while I'm here I visit my first book,
immaculately conceived in such a place,
cells dividing into conference papers
and chapter drafts; the birth bloodless,
leaving no stretch-marks.
An undemanding infant, requiring
no new shoes or orthodontics.

Often I find her snuggled between
"Cyprus from 1191-1374"
and a festschrift for Brenda Bolton,
whose black and white cat
resented posing as partial proof
of the 'human face' of scholarship.

Once when I called she was out.
My heart pricked - well, hermaphrodite,
are you even now fertilizing
a fresh young ovum of discovery
somewhere on the Backs, where swans
twist their necks into lovehearts for the tourists?

'St Deiniol's Library'

Morning

For two hours only, twice that week,
the whiteness of winter sun
illuminates my books, casting
strong shadows on the leather spines
of silent companions,
books which wall me an anchoress
bending over page after page
under a light purified of colour.

My feet relax, surreptitiously,
on the heating pipes which hug
the banisters of the gallery.

Afternoon

Wrapped in my philosopher's scarf
I let the tall door swing shut behind me,
closing me into this other world,
a perspective both vast and intimate
where Stylites lengthen pillars,
post-procreative matrons shun their mates
and hormone-fuelled youths
vacillate, asking "this world - or the next?"

Slippered and shawled, I pad and prowl,
catching unawares a note,
a reference, an elusive thought
hovering almost beyond reach,
like moths which throw themselves
at the disc of light cast on my desk.

I pin them to paper with my pen
and descend to dinner.

Evening

From warming firelight I turn away
seeking again the deep richness
of the book clad room.

Time passes. The darkness muffles
all noise but the staccato click
of fingers on keyboard and creak
of stretching spines.

A farewell symphony plays out
as one by one, each reader dims their lamp:
Narnia-like pools of light waiting
to reappear tomorrow.

'Intelligent Design'

Upgrading from plank-between-pallets
to a proper woodcutter's bench,
squatting, sweating in the act of creation,
screwdriver and wrench to hand
and, having fixed the cross bars (fig 3) onto the legs (fig 5),
I'm musing over the plastic caps
("Stretch tautly over leg ends") and wondering
at just which minute of which hour on the sixth day
God dreamed up the kid's skid-proof hoof
and how many begattings of goats it took
to perfect the angle of their grip.

'Tyddewi revisted'

Someone had just left in a hurry -
God himself, I think - leaving ugly seats
leaning against the slanting purple slate.
I imagine him levering himself
out of the Bishop's throne
and striding down the nave,
brandishing his crook above his head
and roaring imprecations in Welsh
at oblivious pairs of lambs,
all flashing eyes and swirling whiskers
like an arthritic bard, declaiming
'I'm coming home!' as he stumbles
on the footpath to the chapel
rooted on the cliff.
'Leave the door open!' he shouts,
'So the seagull's cry can perch on the altar stones
and the children's prayers float on the crest of the wave,
and let the chairs stand ready
for a weary walker to rest a while,
especially if she can't find the right words
in either language to call me by my name.'
And he swoops off into the sea-mist,
the hem of his robe towed by a kittiwake.

'Square Peg'

The mice are the worst. Rats,
you can get your head round
(if you accept they're vicious brutes
with no morals, and bad breath to boot),
but mice - devious little bastards
and so many of the buggers!
Just as you clamp down on one
up pops another, between the curls
of the bellrope: you'd swear
they were laughing at you.
        Ok, so I'm getting on,
and losing that tooth hasn't improved my looks
(not that the verger's tabby minds a jot)
but I'm still up to the job -
that penny a week to keep me in scraps
is well worth the candle,
ha! The candle ends those vermin chew-
quantities of them - and don't get me started
on how they soil the purificators
(though why the sacristan leaves them
in the tower is beyond me, when
there's that fine linen-fold press for storage).
        The tales I would tell if only I could speak -
not just the messed up linen
but how he carries on with Mistress Anne
from the bakehouse. Fresh muffins my arse!
Any fool can see what *he's* after
(though when you see how enticingly
they rise above her bodice
I s'pose muffin's as good a word as any
for those bubbies).
        Sometimes I think I'm wasted here,

a cathedral rodent catcher
in a Mercian city,
and though that hole in the tower door
isn't a bit too tight for *my* lean flanks
it's getting to be quite a stretch down
to the step, the stone slab that takes you
into the cavernous barn of a place,
the crowds of pilgrims and stallholders,
not to mention the pomp and circumstance,
barely a minute's peace till dusk.
      And another thing - I suspect
they're dissenters. Where will it end?

'Silence in Court'

"Many years!" the courtiers acclaim
(loudest of all the one with a phial
of death-dealing venom up his sleeve),
"Many years to Basil, the great, the holy one!"
The engineer pockets his oily feather,
puffs out his cheeks in relief
as the jewelled lions stretch
their hinged jaws, bang on time
to roar their welcome
to the emperor, the elect one
who opened his eyes in the purple chamber,
swaddled in ritual, suckled with greatness.
The gilded cats thump tasselled tails
on the smooth marble floor.
The procession begins.
          It's Constantinople, around a thousand AD.
The Great Palace is sacred space
because it pertains to the person
of a stocky man with a frivolous younger brother,
Basil the Macedonian, soldier, statesman -
latterly ascetic. Even the silence
in the splendid rooms is holy, protected by

DRING!

          It's Leeds, Festival time, 2013.
On the doorstep, home for a break,
a smiling demi-god in muddy jeans.
Many years I leaped into action
leaving my books to service these young heirs.
Long bath, hot food, clean clothes and he's off
before the Byzantine banquet begins.

22

Silence is sacred, protected back then
by a pompous official in the pay of the court.
Soft-soled, obsequious, he shuffles along
its echoing corridors, parched in the sun.
In my carpeted study, computer keys clack.

'Gledhow Swan Upping'

Last month three adolescent cygnets ducked their heads,
embarrassed by my interest,
and cob and pen circled their brood
with arching necks and coiled wings.
Now two offspring alone remain,
emboldened, perhaps, by the sudden spillage
of growth down the hillside, where bonsai versions
of good green things begin to top the soil,
beguiling the stubborn snow with promises
of celandines, feathery fronds of wood anemones,
and flat blades of bluebells, ramsons, cuckoopint
in promiscuous proximity.

And the dogwalker's accent
conveys an authority at odds with her grimy jacket -
she thinks our missing fledgling's a boy,
that 'dad' has seen him off
so he can 'have another go at mum.'

Unmated now, I yet recall a time
when pairing meant for keeps,
and what I've kept from then I will not lose.
Unlike these swans, no male possessor
will drive away my sons
because the breeding season's come again.

Walking home on ripening soil, my warm breath
ascends in frosty homage to the dryads;
offering thanks for green-ness, sunshine,
thawing snow, wet dogs, wild birds
and gloriously free range sons.

'Sound track'

Pouring scorn on feeble female fumblings
with the sat nav, he suggests
I'm cartographically challenged, too,
not noticing how I'm led by music.
and thus I note my routes.
The A14 turn off the A1 is mostly
at seven and a half minutes into track one
of a certain something by Syd Barrett,
a last shared chord
with the student slumbering beside me,
harvesting his final hour of sleep
before the winter sowing.

Heading north again, safely delivered,
we're empty, the car and I.
Shine on, you crazy diamond,
sparkling in the misty fens.
My insurers must never know
I've been driving under the influence of Pink Floyd.

'Nina knows how'

The epitome of perfect timing
is not breaking bad news so it is heard
or delivering the punchline's meaning
but the lingering between chord and word.
The song floats into silence, a plucked string
with a soft susurration of wire brush,
piano arpeggios - then she will sing,
launching one word, then another - no rush
to reach the cadence; languid pleasuring
of waiting ears by a voice that tingles
your scalp with its teasing delay, gathering
hope and longing, peace and hunger mingled.
'He needs me,' she declares: friend or lover
(demon or god) is yet to discover.

'Ley Lines'

Last Spring was so cold
my feet had flattened the swishing grass
into a route from backdoor to greenhouse
where, coaxed and cosseted,
sprigs of green crowned the soil
long before the first euphoric cut
of summer smoothed the lawn.

And then emerged some primitive tread,
a darker, feral track
crossing my route, scoring the garden
with its pungent directness
at right angles to my puny path.

Right now, mid-afternoon,
the cropped grass intoxicates;
falling blossom and blackbird's call
embrace each other between earth and sky.

The pages rest unturned as senses gather
lilac blossom, wallflowers, cloudless sky,
the intrusive percussion of a power drill,
a spider negligently traversing one bared foot.

But sometimes at the margins of the day
I spot the fox who pursues his power line,
his nose raised and focused on an ancient task.
Unabashed he takes undeviating aim.

'Cormorant'

Almost all blackish, with a good deal of gloss,
favouring the Black and Caspian Seas
(also West Greenland and Sardinia).
Partial migrant in Europe, breeds
sometimes together with herons in high trees,
sometimes in reed beds. Nests
consisting of sticks, also seaweed.

There is a sharply demarcated white patch
on cheeks and chins (distinguishing them
from shags). Sexually mature
at three years, immatures
have whitish underparts; in summer
a white patch appears on the thighs.

Some have whitish underparts, both male
and female almost all blackish
(with a good deal of gloss).
Some have whitish heads.
A white patch appears on the thighs.

In summer sometimes in reed beds
and sometimes in high trees.
Its wintering areas are the western and Mediterranean areas.

Single-brooded, breeds colonially, nests
with a finer lining (but sticks, also seaweed).
Predominantly fish, especially eels,
eels caught by diving while swimming,
sometimes in reed beds and
sometimes in high trees.

Partial migrant, single-brooded, almost all blackish.

A sonorous 'chrochrochro' with manifold variations
as well as croaking and hissing noises may be heard
at the nest site. Sharply demarcated,
croaking and hissing,
whitish parts may be found.

Seaweed sonorous, eels swimming.

'Neti, neti'

Not black, not green,
Not purple, not blue,
Magpie feather spearing the grass,
Weightless dart defying the lawnmower.
I've misjudged you, raucous visitor –
Not bully, not villain, not cock of the roost
Though you lord it over song birds.
No human technology could frame
the steely tapered rib
Or weave ten lustrous shades in one.
You're not so clever, for all your bluster
And without this feather
A pinhead of fear lodges inside you.
What is your end to be?
Not this, not that,
Fox, human, cat.
Not ever, not yet.

'Off the leash'

I'm taking this poem for a walk, because
Billy Collins says dogs write in poetry,
so I wind a retracting lead round my wrist
and off we go. Sniff at that stone,
piss on the bushes – nothing yet.
But as I climb a stile, look –
the tight coils of a sonnet
slithering into the long grass.
Reaching for the plumpest blackberry – plop!
A juicy synonym drops into my hand.
Off the leash, and suddenly we're in a sports car,
driving with the top down, grinning inanely
through oversized shades,
your feathery ears and my wild hair
pennants in the breeze.
          We're back, towelled dry and watered.
As I approach my desk, two limpid eyes
bore into my back. What? You want to go out?
Again? Well, don't be long!

Acknowledgments

This collection of poetry was compiled and produced as a project for an MA in Creative Writing undertaken at Leeds Trinity University under the much valued guidance of poets and performing artists Oz Hardwick (author of *The Kind Ghosts* (bluechrome, 2004), *Carrying Fire* (bluechrome, 2006), *The Lost Songs* (Indigo Dreams, 2009), *The Illuminated Dreamer* (Oversteps, 2010) and *An Eschatalogical Bestiary* (Dog Horn, 2013)) and Amina Alyal (who has published poetry in anthologies and journals, including the *Aesthetica Creative Writing Annual 2013*, *Pressed by Unseen Feet*, ed. Rose Drew and Alan Gillot (Stairwell Books 2012) and *Envoi*, Issue 166, November 2013).)The module co-ordinator was prose writer Martyn Bedford. Many thanks are due to them and to my co-conspirator and fellow student, Maria Preston. Together we established this Imprint to publish the work of Leeds Trinity University postgraduates. It sits alongside a regular Open Mic event in Horsforth known as *Wordspace*, the title devised by Rosemary Mitchell. Thanks are also due to Susan Anderson for facilitating this and permitting the use of that 'brand' to provide an integrated platform for the written and performed word arising from the Creative Writing programmes at Leeds Trinity University. Much appreciation is due to local poets I have met and worked with in recent years, including Joy Howard and James Nash.

Thanks are also due to all those people who inspire, read and respond to my poetry and who share in my other lives, in which I am a hill-walker, gardener, singer, cat-owner and scholar of Eastern Christianity. Special thanks to Suzanne Owen for allowing me to use her photos for the cover images.

Notes

'Algebra' was first published by Caught in the Net, Issue 130, March 2014. *Humphrey Head* is a nature reserve near Morecombe Bay, reputedly where the last wolf in England was killed. The title of 'Vegetable Love' is an allusion to Andrew Marvell's 'To His Coy Mistress.' He is one of the Metaphysical poets. 'Book of Hours' refers to the Medieval prayer books of the monastic 'hours' or services; they were often lavishly illustrated with secular imagery. A Palimpsest is a manuscript written over another scratched out manuscript. Discalced Carmelites are a religious order who go barefoot or in sandals. Byzantinists are scholars of the Eastern Christian Empire which fell to the Turks in 1453. North front, floor four is a location within Cambridge University Library; 'the Backs' is the waterway that runs behind some of the colleges in the city. St Deniol's library, now renamed Gladstone's library, is a residential library in Flintshire. Anchoresses were hermits who chose to be walled into cells attached to churches; Stylites were ascetics who chose to spend their lives standing on pillars; Haydn's 'Farewell symphony' was written out of sympathy for court musicians who were being denied breaks: one by one they extinguished their candles and left the orchestra pit so that the symphony ended with just one instrument playing. Purificators are small cloths used in the Eucharist service. The Swan Upping is an annual ceremony that takes place on the Thames, in which the Queen's swans are counted. 'Comorant' is a 'found' poem using words taken from the Collins Colour Guide to Birds. 'Neti, neti' is a phrase from Hindu religion, meaning 'not this, not that'.

Index of first lines page

Printed in Germany
by Amazon Distribution
GmbH, Leipzig